From Happy Dog to Dolly Parton

Reflections on a Christian life

by Chris Thomas

Spring View Publications

SpringViewPublications@outlook.com

Copyright © Chris Thomas 2016

Typeset by Candy Evans, Kenilworth
Cover image by Andrew Ditton
Cover design by Roy Broomhead

Printed and bound by IngramSpark
www.ingramspark.com

ISBN **978-1-5262-0311-3**

Foreward

I was pleased to be asked to write a few words about Chris on the occasion of his 80th birthday.

We first met in the early 1960s as neighbours on a new housing development outside Tonbridge in Kent. He and Daphne worshipped at the Baptist Church in town, whilst we attended the local Anglican mission church in the next road. I think probably the only thing that separated us as Christians was the amount of water needed for baptisms!

A shared experience of tragedy, when we both lost young children, drew us closer together. In those dark days our faith was severely tested, but we found God to be a rock on whom we could depend, whose love surrounded and upheld us.

Over the years, during which Chris became a Reader in the Church of England and I was ordained, we have supported each other through an extended network of prayer, in times of both sadness and joy.

Chris's articles reflect his deep faith, combined with an imaginative and delightful sense of humour. We hope there will be many more to come, and that they will continue to encourage and challenge those who read them.

Revd John Pelley

Introduction

This book contains the first 50 of my father's 'snippets', as he calls them, written over the last three years for the website of St John's Church, Kenilworth, Warwickshire. They have been inspired by around 60 years of faith and reflect many of the stories that have graced my father's sermons over the years and inspired many people in their Christian journeys.

Thanks are due to Revd Andrew Attwood, vicar of St John's, for encouraging my father to put fingers to keyboard so others can share these thoughts. It is my privilege to present them to a different audience in print to celebrate his 80th birthday.

The original snippets, along with some new ones, can be found online at

www.stjohnschurchkenilworth.org.uk

I hope and pray you also find encouragement in these pages.

Candy Evans

May 2016

Baby, you've changed ...

Many things about the modern world are mystifying to my generation. For example, nowadays there are doors in public places that bear the legend BABY CHANGING ROOM. I've sat drinking coffee and observed parents taking bundles into these rooms and noticed to my bafflement that they always come out with the same baby. So what's the point?

If they were dissatisfied with the baby's looks or behaviour, why not take advantage of what appears to be a free exchange system?

Maybe it's not so simple. After all, most of us would like to effect some fundamental change in our nearest and dearest, but there's always some hindrance. It used to be said that every bride at her wedding muttered the mantra 'aisle, altar, hymn' – think about it – only to find that what she expected to change was actually the essence of the person with whom she'd fallen in love. An essence that couldn't and shouldn't be changed.

I know there's a lot about me I'd dearly love to change, but I'd have as little chance of success as I would trying to change anybody else. There's a promise of total change for all of us who believe. Paul wrote "We eagerly await ... the Lord Jesus Christ, who ... will transform our lowly bodies so that they will be like his glorious body." Philippians 3:20,21. The trouble is that will be in heaven, which could be a long time to wait (or not, as the case may be).

Meanwhile what can we do to change those aspects of ourselves that don't fit what we know of God's way? Well, actually, it's been done already. Paul again: "Our old self was crucified with Jesus." Romans 6:6

He's done it for us, so all we need to do is give ourselves into his care. Maybe we need a notice on the church door reading PEOPLE CHANGING ROOM.

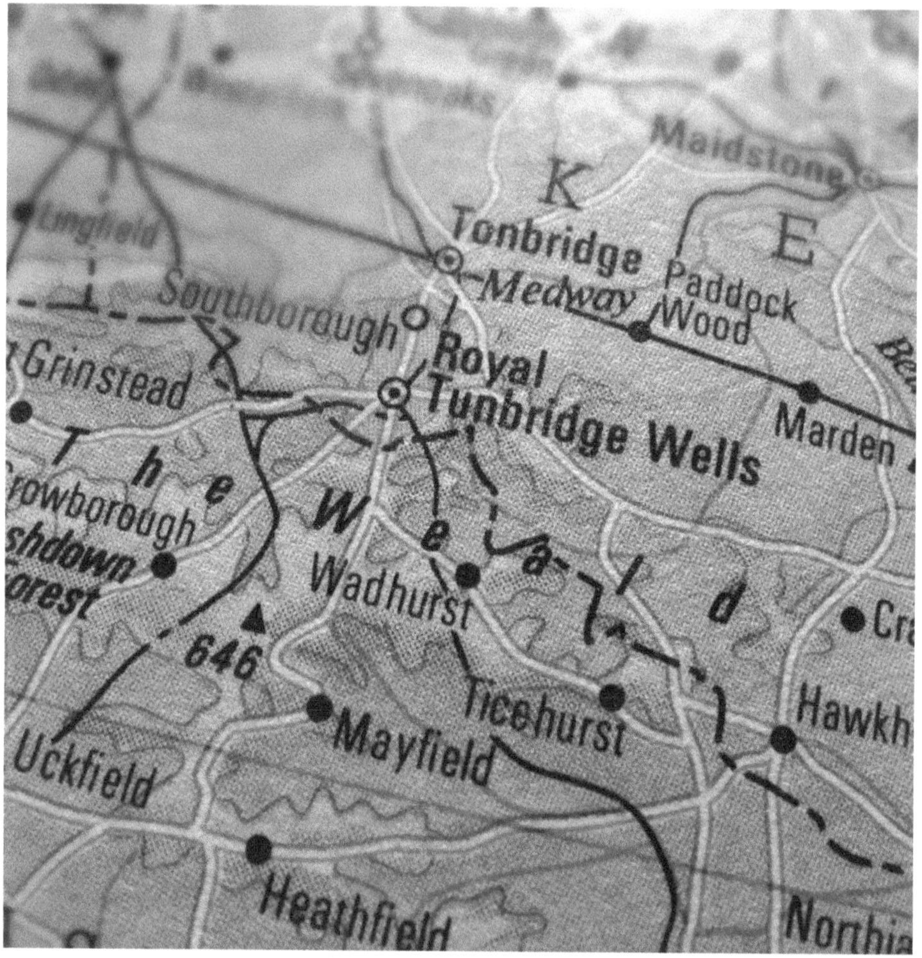
Maidstone
K
E
Tonbridge
Paddock
Wood
Medway
Southborough
Royal
Tunbridge Wells
Marden
Grinstead
The Weald
rowborough
shdown
orest
Wadhurst
646
Ticehurst
Hawkh
Mayfield
Uckfield
Heathfield
Northia

Little things mean a lot

In my Sunday School days it was the practice to ask "What's your favourite Bible verse?" You were expected to come out with the great truths of the faith, like John 3:16 or Matthew 28:20, but my favourite has always been "He that blesseth his friend with a loud voice, rising early in the morning, it shall be counted a curse to him." Proverbs 27:14. It sounds more menacing in the King James Version.

We spend much time trying to communicate the Big Ideas of God's love, Jesus' sacrifice, the indwelling of the Spirit, but easily forget the little ways in which we should be showing the outworking of the Big Ideas in everyday life.

Not long after we moved to Kent, my wife held a shop door open for a Typical Tunbridge Wells Lady, who regarded her quizzically and said "You're not from round here, are you?" Little acts of courtesy or kindness were obviously rare, so my wife stood out – perhaps more than if she'd loudly proclaimed the Gospel on the street corner.

The very first miracle Jesus is recorded as performing, at the wedding in Cana (John 2) was a simple act of courtesy. To save the host embarrassment when the wine ran out, Jesus changed the water into a fine vintage. Not ostentatiously, but quietly, so that life was made simpler for the host, and nobody need ever know.

Blessing your neighbour is a wonderful thing, but not at full volume at 6am. Showing God's love in the little things should come naturally to us the closer we get to Jesus, and we should take care not to neglect them. St David of Wales taught his followers to "Be joyful, keep the faith and do the little things you have seen me do". Love in the little things – perhaps there is no better way to introduce anyone to Jesus.

Say what you mean

Being hard of hearing is a good excuse to use the subtitles on TV, which can be a delight when they get it wrong. Recently in a report about a new medical treatment the subtitles said that the procedure would "avoid the need for evasive surgery". Obviously they meant "invasive surgery", but it set me wondering what evasive surgery might be.

I suppose a surgeon who couldn't face a patient needing an organ transplant could dodge the issue by pretending to concentrate on his toenails instead, but it stretches the imagination. We expect medics to be straight with us, but nice with it, not frightening or bullying or offhand.

What about our own dealings with others? Each week in church we (are supposed to) learn more about Jesus, but are we ready to take a cue from him when people ask us about our faith?

I remember only too well, many years ago, sitting in the bar of a Tel Aviv hotel with a colleague who suddenly asked me: "You've got a faith, haven't you? What does it mean to you?" I choked on my pizza and mumbled something about a personal God and doing good to others. I was shamefully unready.

Now Jesus was always ready, and direct, and sensitive. A rich young man asked about eternal life, and Jesus gave it to him straight but gently – and he went away sad (Matthew 19:22). A disreputable woman drawing water from a well also got more than she bargained for when she asked about living water, then ran to tell everyone: "Come, see a man who told me everything I ever did. Could this be the Christ?" John 4:29

A subtly different approach to each person, but a clear unmistakable message that made an impact. No evasive surgery there. As for us, speaking on his behalf, the best thing is to be prepared, so it's worth practising our own story so that we have it ready when needed. As Peter wrote: "Always be prepared to give an answer to everyone who asks you to give the reason for the hope that you have." 1 Peter 3:15

Beware trolleys

Unexpected perils dwell in the innocent surroundings of Waitrose car park. Have you noticed the admonition on each shopping trolley that says "This trolley will stop suddenly if you try to leave the facility"? Disturbing!

First of all, I didn't know I was in a Facility – I thought it was a supermarket car park. Facility sounds like a mysterious installation in the Nevada desert that officially doesn't exist.

Then "Stop suddenly"? What about if I've emptied the trolley into the car boot and passed it to somebody else – as I drive out of the Facility, will the trolley Stop Suddenly by the Ready Meals, throwing its elderly female driver head first into the Vegetable Lasagne?

The problem is that we expect instant and terrible retribution if we break or even slightly bend the law, and if it doesn't happen we get round to thinking that maybe the law isn't so important after all.

The Jews of Old Testament times had a simple and sensible set of laws from God, around which they built a web of lesser rules to which they stuck in fear of dreadful punishment from him. Woe betide anybody who disregarded the rules, because the priests would come down like a ton of bricks, even if God didn't.

Jesus boiled it all down to a much simpler formula: love God, and love your neighbour (Mark 12:29-31). What mattered, he said, wasn't the letter of the law but the motivation behind our words and actions (Matthew 5:27, 28), and in any case the law had been useful for humanity in its infancy, but now we have Jesus, who had come to fulfil the law (Matthew 5:17). If non-believers tell us we follow nonsensical rules, we can respond that if we want to be like Jesus it comes naturally to want to love as he does, and life's trolley won't Stop Suddenly if we get things wrong once in a while.

Remember me

One of the people I knew at university later became a Famous Film Star. Naturally we lost touch, and I have no lurid stories of Hollywood Babylon to share.

One odd incident, however, is worth retelling. Nearly thirty years after we'd left university a TV company decided to feature him in a "This Is Your Life" programme. He had been in a student production of Shakespeare in 1958, so they tried to restage scenes from that production as a filmed insert to the live programme that would be broadcast from California.

They rounded up the play's producer and three of the original cast members, including me, and got us together in the college grounds. Now I remember it being lovely weather in 1958, but the producer said he definitely remembered snow. So on a freezing February day they erected a huge wind machine into which they threw bits of expanded polystyrene to represent a snowstorm. It was so cold, and I quietly cursed the producer's memory. I'm still sure he was mistaken.

We depend so much on memory. The Jews to this day build their Passover ritual round recital of the good things God has done for them, so nobody will ever forget.

We too build our Communion service round Jesus' command to "do this in remembrance of me" (Luke 22:19), and we could say the whole of the Gospel message is contained in the words "Remember me".

But let's not forget it works both ways. We try to remember him, while he never forgets us. He's the God who said "you are precious and honoured in my sight, and I love you" (Isa 43:4). No matter how alone or lost we feel, we can always turn to Jesus, like the thief on the next-door cross, ask him to "remember me" and be sure of a warm and loving response.

Unlike my friend the Famous Film Star. When they showed the filmed reconstruction during the live programme, his face was a total blank – he remembered nothing about it. Thank God that he never forgets us.

Pig Pong

At our last family get-together all was peaceful and respectable until somebody suggested Pig Pong. If you've never played Pig Pong, I suggest it should be avoided by those of a nervous disposition. Like Table Tennis, it requires a net dividing a table, across which pairs or individuals face each other. However instead of a ball you play with an insubstantial construct of feather-light plastic, and instead of a bat each player has a hollow rubber pig.

The object is to keep the "ball" in the air by squeezing your pig, thus emitting a puff of air. Eventually it falls on one side or the other, to the delight of the player whose pig has puffed most vigorously. It's a hugely enjoyable pastime, involving as it does our favourite activity of keeping a subject in the air by producing as much hot air as possible.

Conversations after church services can be much like this – essential bonding between members of the Body of Christ, while actually being little more than exchanging puffs of air.

Does it happen in home groups, do you think? We bandy about serious concepts like salvation, grace, forgiveness, but how often do we simply keep them up in the air to avoid having to let them come down on our side of the net and do something about them?

Great puffs of words are fun, but not much use on their own: "When words are many, sin is not absent, but he who holds his tongue is wise." Proverbs 10:19

Sermons can be gloriously inspiring (trust me, I'm a Reader), but how often do we come away feeling we're on a high that will fade before long, and at a loss about what to do? When I was in training my wise Vicar told me to finish my sermons by "always giving them something to DO". We need to anchor the great truths of our faith in practical action, or as James put it "Do not merely listen to the word ... do what it says." James 1:22

The ball will fall in our court at some point. Let's be ready with action rather than hot air.

I've got an app for that

They're creeping in everywhere, and nobody seems to realise that our lives are being taken over. That innocent mobile phone can tell you when to get out of bed, how to get to Auntie Flo's, the best way to cook eggs à la Delia Smith, etc etc etc ...

Is it any wonder that we are becoming a nation of couch potatoes when we don't need to stir from the sofa, because there are apps to handle any domestic emergency?

Of course there are good things about it. Humanity has never had such instant access to a vast cloud of information, and using an app does (or should) free up time for more interesting and important things. But I do feel a sense of loss about the thrill of the chase. If we've got an app to do it for us, why bother to work it out ourselves?

Take family history research. Nowadays it's so easy. Via the internet, you can become related to King Canute in an afternoon, and then forget all about it. When I started my quest around 1970, all you had were the dusty, barely decipherable original documents, but they engendered a passion for the hunt, a deep engagement to the extent that once I shocked the other occupants of the National Archives by bawling "Yes!" when an unexpected entry blew me away.

How do we find out about God? Is there an app for that? There's a great temptation to accept the views of other, older, wiser people and not ask any of the fundamental questions that really bother us. We're told that God intended X, or Jesus meant Y, and who are we to disagree?

It's fine as far as it goes, but Paul reprimands his friends in Corinth for being content with milk when he wants to give them "solid food" (1 Corinthians 2). To know Jesus must involve digging deeper, asking awkward questions, ferreting away until we know and experience Jesus personally.

In this life we'll never be fully satisfied, but oh boy, it's fun finding out! Just be ready for the baffled looks when you shout out "Yes!" in the Cathedral, or wherever it happens!

You talking to me?

I always thought our present Queen invented the royal walkabout in Australia in 1970, but it seems that Queen Victoria was ahead of her.

Anyway, I was told that Victoria was the one involved in the story about a small child in the crowd at some royal event, who when approached by a rather dumpy but august figure was heard to say "Go away Queen, I'm eating my banana". Come to think of it, if it was indeed Victoria then a banana was a rare exotic treat, and worthy of one's full attention.

Every day we are faced with decisions on priority. Read the newspaper or mow the lawn? Go now to see the boss or surreptitiously check your emails in case a certain person has agreed to go on a date? Or more fundamentally, philosophical dilemmas like the TV advert in which a small girl was asked by her sister "Which is better – Daddy or chips?" I can't remember what product was being advertised, but the problem haunts me. How to decide which should have priority?

There are plenty of examples in the Bible of people hearing God's voice, often at very inconvenient moments. No wonder the response was often "Lord, here am I – please send somebody else". But at least most of them recognised who was talking to them. In our noise-filled world it's more difficult both to hear him and to know whose message it is.

Even when we have a Quiet Time and listen hard, the busyness of the day crowds our thoughts. And God speaks to each of us in different ways: to some he's loud and dramatic and impossible to mistake, while to others it's more like Elijah's "gentle whisper." 1 Kings 19:12

I seem to get God's messages mainly through other people. At Spring Harvest not long ago one of the Saltmine drama team and the pastor and writer Jeff Lucas both said the same thing to me, using the same words. I reckon that must have been from God. What we need is to be alert to hear him, and to give top priority to the message.

Other priorities follow on: Jesus said "Seek first his kingdom ... and all these things will be given to you as well" (Matthew 6:33). Bananas will be provided!

Happy Dog

Living as we do on a main road in an elderly house with low-set windows, we can enjoy observing humanity while sipping our morning tea. Every day there come the dog-walkers, for each of whose animals we have a nickname.

The one we look forward to most is the one we call Happy Dog. I'll not describe him to protect anonymity, but what is so striking is his huge enjoyment of every moment. His tail wags like there's no tomorrow, he darts to and fro to explore new smells (many of them his own from the day before), he glances cheerfully at his master and trots willingly where he's told to go, all the time wearing a beatific expression of sheer joy. Life is rich and full, and he savours every second of it.

That's what Jesus promised us: he said he had come so that we might "have life, and have it to the full" (John 10:10). On another occasion he said "I have told you this so that my joy may be in you and that your joy may be complete." John 15:11

There's a common misconception that if you're a Christian you ought to be in a permanent state of Happy Dog, bounding merrily through life. Didn't Paul exhort his readers to "Be joyful always" (1 Thessalonians 5:16)? At the very least we shouldn't be like a friend of ours who was once described as "Old 'I've got joy unspeakable'", said with a thoroughly miserable expression.

Christians are the same as everybody; life brings bad times, and who knows that better than Jesus? We can boil over with anger and frustration and still be loved unconditionally by God. What we need to aim for is a solid core of certainty and wonder and love, created by the presence of the Holy Spirit in us, fed by prayer and fellowship and the Word, to carry us through whatever may happen.

By all means let's overflow with worship and revel in our joy, but let's not put on a false air of rejoicing when it's obviously not feasible.

As for me, I just want to enjoy God's world like Happy Dog, uncomplicated and full of promise.

Woof!

Stairway to heaven?

For a number of years I worked just off Oxford Street in London, a few hundred yards from Selfridge's, which naturally became a good place to wander round in brief lunch breaks. Just one thing disturbed the luxury of this temple of consumerism. As you approached the escalator, you were faced with a notice that said "CARRY DOGS AND PUSHCHAIRS".

This was the early 1960s, when big stores could afford to be peremptory with customers, and I always felt guilty when heading for the escalator. I didn't have a dog to hand, and was not yet at a stage of life to have access to a pushchair, so how could I be entitled to use the escalator? Sneakily, I sometimes did (and got away with it), but more often clumped up the echoing stairway instead.

We have enough trouble believing that we are worthy enough to travel God's UP escalator, without adding to the list of things required before we even set foot on it. Surely God didn't offer an open invitation to just anybody to begin the assisted climb to his kingdom of glorious promise?

Well, yes, he did, actually, and goes on doing so.

Don't we have to be extra-pious and squeaky clean to present ourselves?

No – we just have to be ourselves, sinful and weak and unreliable and doubting and incoherent and unready and everything you'd expect to disqualify us from admittance to God's presence.

Moreover, that's ALL we have to be – as useless as that, but prepared to offer ourselves to him unconditionally. People may tell us we have to be baptised in a certain way, to use particular language when talking to God, to go to church at least twice every Sunday (properly dressed, of course), and almost anything that adds to the hurdles between us and knowing God.

Ignore them! Ignore anything that says we need Jesus AND this or that. If we acknowledge our sinfulness, then all we need is Jesus, who has cleared away every obstacle: "We have peace with God through our Lord Jesus Christ, through whom we have gained access by faith into this grace in which we now stand." Romans 5:1,2. Put down the dog and the pushchair and just step out in faith on God's escalator, and see where it takes you!

So what do you expect?

One member of our extended family is a very likeable character, with a nice line in sardonic humour, but has never been one for the noisy (sometimes forced) enjoyments of big family gatherings. To him, party games and the like are a subtle form of torture. So it was with surprise that one Christmas I heard him say: "I've just realised I've been bored for two whole hours without noticing it!" For once, the fun had far exceeded his expectations.

Maybe he's right not to expect too much, so he won't be disappointed – but that attitude tends to make life pretty unexciting and, in the end, pointless. Perhaps we need to expect something, but not too much, just in case?

For instance, when did you last set off for Church on a Sunday expecting to be blown away by the experience? Or did you think "same old, same old," because that's how things usually work out?

The trouble is we tend to expect everything to be laid out for us, in bite-sized pieces, so we can go away happily replete without having to make any effort. It's Ready Meal religion that really suits us.

Of course there will be times when we're too drained to expect anything, and it's often then that God surprises us with love. But otherwise if we want to benefit from worship we need at the very least to cultivate a mindset of expectation.

The disciples didn't drop everything and follow Jesus just because he seemed a nice bloke, they saw he promised a new life, a life full of the unexpected, and that's what they needed.

All of our faith is based on expectation. As Paul says (Romans 8:19) "Creation waits in eager expectation" for God to fulfil the astounding promises he's given us.

Let's go to our next service or home group, not expecting to be bored for an hour or so, but ready to receive, react, respond, and rejoice in the unexpected gifts of God. And then perhaps we can be ready for whatever unexpected thing God wants to do with us.

"Nobody" said Monty Python "expects the Spanish Inquisition", and it was a damp squib when it came, but every Christian can expect the unexpected, every day.

You CAN take it with you

"What does that notice mean?" said my travelling companion. "I'm sure it said 'Portable Riverside'." It was yellow, and prominent, and intriguing. Then I saw it too through the bus window.

It read "Portobello, Riverside" and pointed to a new housing development.

Disappointing, really, because I rather like the idea of a Portable Riverside. Just imagine relaxing on the bank, water lapping at your feet, the occasional plash from a passing rowboat or a foraging water vole, a chain of ducklings snuggling in behind Ma Mallard, dragonflies shimmering among the bullrushes ... so idyllic, you wish you could parcel it up and take it with you everywhere. Now if only there were a Portable Riverside, life might be easier to bear.

Unfortunately we tend to leave the Riverside behind and let our minds dwell on today's worries and fears, letting all the scum of daily pressure rise to the surface.

That's surely not how God wants us to live. Jesus told us not to worry (Matthew 6:34) but to live life to the full (John 10:10). This means taking a break by the riverside every now and then – as Jesus did in the restful environment of Martha and Mary's house (Luke 10:38-42) – and holding in our minds the Riverside in all its beauty – as John paints the Eternal City in the book called Revelation.

The Riverside is always there for us to enjoy, and at any moment we can be there, sitting with Jesus and enjoying the world he created for us.

It's not surprising Psalm 23 is so popular: "He maketh me to lie down in green pastures: he leadeth me beside the still waters ..." It sums up all we need to remember when we desperately long for peace and quiet.

And in answer to those who say our faith is a "comfort blanket", Psalm 23 doesn't dodge the nastiness of life (the valley of the shadow of death), but just reminds us of the permanence of God's presence and love – "my rock" as the psalmist calls him (Psalm 62), always there regardless of what happens in the world, always pointing onwards to the glory of the Kingdom to come.

Next time you see the sign, head for Portable Riverside!

Weebles wobble ...

"Weebles wobble but they don't fall down" - remember the slogan?

In our household when the children were small we built up a fair collection of these egg-shaped figures, which because of their weighted hemispherical base did indeed always return to the upright position no matter what you did to them.

Later on I kept one on my desk at work, as a diagnostic tool. I would find that when discussion of a problem had gone round in circles for too long, all I had to do was spin the Weeble, and the person at whom it was staring when it came to rest was responsible for sorting the problem out. Visiting dignitaries were sometimes puzzled to see a toy on the desk of a senior manager in the public service, but it proved as good a problem-solving tool as anything else.

Difficulties in life so often don't have any obvious solution. Do Christians have better ways of sorting themselves out? It's instructive to look at the book of Acts, and the giving of the Holy Spirit at Pentecost. Before that day the disciples often drew lots to make decisions. Afterwards the Spirit is invoked every time.

For us nowadays it's crucial to remember to get God involved, as the epistle of James spells out with typical directness in chapter 4 verses 13-17. Jesus said: "by myself I can do nothing" (John 5:30), and we too should automatically rely on the ultimate source of advice and clarity.

When we face big (or little) decisions of course we need to consider all the pros and cons – God expects us to use the brains he gave us – but then share them with him in prayer, being ready to do what he says no matter how off the wall it may seem to us. The answer can come in many different ways.

Just occasionally there may be no obvious answer, so we have to use what we know of the character of God as a template against which to measure what we decide to do. Provided we spend enough time with him in prayer or reading his word, we can't go far wrong.

After all, Weebles wobble like all of us do, but in the end they won't fall down.

Be like the Gutbucket Five

Albert Wynn was born in 1907, and the few existing fragments of his work were recorded in the late 1920s and early '30s. I have one precious gramophone record (10inch, 78rpm) of "After you've gone" by Albert Wynn and his Gutbucket Five, a recording that seems to have escaped the notice of the chroniclers of early jazz – better known is "Parkway Stomp" by the Gutbucket Seven.

Yes, all right, I'm a geek so far as New Orleans jazz and its derivatives are concerned, to the extent of only reluctantly accepting the inclusion of the saxophone into the traditional cornet – trombone – clarinet – rhythm line-up.

In the music world today what counts is often the celebrity status of a musician rather than his or her musicianship. Appearance on "The X Factor" matters, whereas a joy of early jazz was the ensemble work. Each member of the group aspired to be a virtuoso on his (rarely her) instrument but concentrated on making glorious sounds together with the others, all improvising around a chord sequence. Every now and then a player would play a sparkling solo but then merge back into the band. People like Louis Armstrong were both brilliant soloists and essential contributors to the overall sound.

Paul in his letters makes several references to the Body of Christ, and how each one of us is part of that body: "in Christ we, though many, form one body, and each member belongs to all the others." (Romans 12:5). He goes on to talk about each of us having different but complementary gifts. That doesn't seem to give much opportunity for the development of self-expression or individuality, but we should take this alongside Jesus' assertion that he had come so that we "may have life, and have it to the full." John 10:10

So as members of the Body of Christ we not only fulfil our role as an essential component of the body, but also develop the skills and aptitudes God has given us as much as we can, to his glory.

Why "Gutbucket"? It was a little tin bucket hung on the spigot of a liquor barrel to catch the precious drips. Even the humblest of us has a part to play, and play very well, with God's help.

London Borough of Southwark

The Clink
1151-1780

Most notorious
medieval prison

Voted by the People

A green plaque

They've put a commemorative plaque on the wall of our old house in Kent.

Not a blue one, like the national ones saying "John Keats lived here", but a green one, affixed by the local community. We sold our house to a very nice man, a retired senior diplomat and Knight of the Realm, who had been deeply involved in the town and was a well-liked President of the local Civic Society. When he died four years later, it was only natural to put up a memorial recording his sojourn in the (very ordinary) house during the years 2000 to 2004. Drinks and nibbles were consumed on the small front lawn.

But – hang on a moment – doesn't our occupation of the house from 1968 to 2000 merit some recognition? Where's the plaque telling the world we'd lived there for more than 30 years?

Maybe we just didn't make enough of a mark on local society. Friends will remember us, but we have no right to expect preferential treatment just because we were there.

There's a little story in Matthew's Gospel (Matthew 20:20-23) in which the mother of James and John, clearly a Pushy Mum, asks Jesus to promise her sons might sit at his right and left in the Kingdom. Jesus gently responds that (a) it's not in his gift, but God's; (b) she doesn't know what she's asking – it would carry fearsome obligations; (c) status isn't what counts in God's world. "Whoever wants to be first must be your slave – just as the Son of Man did not come to be served, but to serve."

Like so many of Jesus' teachings, this is directly opposed to what we normally expect. Human society teaches us the loudest voice prevails, ambition is essential, we must aim higher, and Look After Number One.

Jesus gives us a simple rule of life: love God, and love our neighbour. Do that, and life becomes better for all of us.

If a plaque was fixed to my house, I hope I'd be satisfied with "Somebody lived here to whom God said 'Well done, good and faithful servant.'"
Matthew 25:21

That's an ambition worth having.

Decaf religion

The Rector looked after his staff well and we Lay Readers felt pleasantly replete after a good meal at the Rectory. "Coffee, anyone?" It was late in the evening, so I asked: "Do you have decaf?" "Oh," said he dismissively "It's all decaf".

What, all of it? Tea, coffee, cocoa, all with the basic oomph removed? But often we willingly drift into a caffeine-free faith, perhaps without realising it. What brought us to belief in the first place? Most frequently, the testimony of a friend, or attending a Christian gathering where we suddenly found what we'd been looking for, and so on.

What did we find? Comfort, reassurance, fellowship – maybe, too, a new perspective on life and understanding of our part in God's plan. All wonderful and desirable, but only part of the story.

The Victorian child growing up might have been happy with the image of "gentle Jesus, meek and mild", but it can't have helped much in the "dark satanic mills" later on. We rejoice in the mysterious bounty of God's grace and forgiveness, and relax in the warmth of his love, but we too easily sideline the tougher parts of our faith. After all "gentle Jesus meek and mild" was the same person who trashed the money-changers' stalls. Who cursed the unproductive fig tree. Who said things to authority figures that really hit home. Who said "I did not come to bring peace, but a sword." Matthew 10:34

Believing in Jesus carries with it the commitment to follow his lead. That means showing love to the unlovable, speaking out against injustice, going wherever and whenever he tells us to go, leaving behind the ties of money and possessions and even family, and putting his word as our top priority. Jesus called it "taking up his cross." Matthew 10:38

My religion wouldn't be worth much if it were just meek and mild – decaffeinated. It's tough, exhausting, sometimes painful, but it carries unspeakably glorious rewards. It's an adventure, it takes us to unexpected places, but we know he's been there ahead of us and not merely survives but stands by us at every turn: "I am with you always, to the very end of the age." Matthew 28:20

That's enough caffeine to fuel me for life. Are you content with decaf?

Advance, friend

I hear that the great Dolly Parton, Country and Western singer, was being interviewed about her life, and talked about her huge and widespread family. She said that all her cousins were so different from each other that she reckoned every type of human personality was represented. And that meant, she said with a smile, that "I never meet a stranger!"

Not all of us are (or think we are) good at meeting new people. We worry we might say the wrong thing, mortally offend the other person, or (even worse?) give the wrong impression of ourselves.

For Christians there's an additional hurdle, because we're supposed to make a point of getting to know new people in order to tell them the good news about Jesus. He didn't appear to have a problem – Jesus talked to anybody and everybody. Rich entrepreneur or rough labourer smelling of fish, dodgy money-grabber or disreputable foreign slut – all were potential friends.

We need, like him, to cultivate the habit of reaching out to strangers. Far from being a risky business in which we might get hurt, the odds are that we will be richer by getting to know them: "Remember always to welcome strangers, for by doing this, some people have entertained angels without knowing it." Hebrews 13:2, Jerusalem Bible

It feels like a fearsome responsibility. But if we have a go it's amazing how easy it can be.

He even supplies the words to say: "I have put my words in your mouth." Isaiah 51:16

After all, we ought to get to know members of our family, and the Bible emphasises that because of what Jesus did we're all children of God: "You are no longer foreigners and aliens, but fellow-citizens with God's people and members of God's household." Ephesians 2:19

And funnily enough, despite first impressions, basically we all have that family resemblance because we're made in the image of God (Genesis 9:6).

Like Dolly, we'll never meet a stranger.

Well met!

It was a magnificent find – gold and silver artefacts from the Dark Ages, worth many thousands – and as usual any profits from the discovery would be split between the finder and the landowner. The latter was a straightforward farmer, a bit bedazzled by his sudden fame. The TV interviewer asked what had impressed him most about the whole business. He thought for a moment, then with a big smile said "I did meet Gary Lamport!"

Gary (not his real name) was a well-liked reporter on the local TV news. National fame, untold riches, a glimpse into the wealth of the distant past, and the most important thing was that he met Gary.

Every now and then you meet people who are full of the breathless story of how they first met Jesus. Perhaps it was in a dramatic vision like Paul on the Damascus road (Acts 9:3-8) or John on Patmos (Revelation 1:12-19), and that sort of story makes us think that's what we should expect.

But when you talk to Christians you find much more varied experience. Some desperately want to meet him, but find he's not quite what they expect, like the rich young man in Luke 18:18-23. Others

are curious and want to catch a glimpse of him but try to keep out of sight (perhaps like Zacchaeus in Luke 19:1-10), then find themselves drawn in by his love.

But by far the majority of people who met Jesus in the Gospels did so in the business of an ordinary day, and that's still the case today. We can meet him in the words or actions of a colleague, in a news story about a deed of love, in a phrase that leaps out of a Bible reading, in the words of a song – and if we are alert we can recognise him for who he is and welcome him as a friend.

Unless of course we'd rather not. It's entirely our choice.

Look back on today. Did we meet him? Were we sufficiently awake to the possibility? Or was the attraction of fame or riches more important at that moment?

He's always there. We need to be ready to meet him in the unexpected and recognise the importance of that meeting above all else.

Is there anybody there?

A small boy of our acquaintance went on a school trip to the seaside. Home again, he was bursting to tell his mother about the moment when a seagull made a mess on the teacher's head. "Oh dear," she said, "What did he say?"

"He didn't say anything, he just flewed away."

History doesn't record the teacher's reaction.

Despite all the promises in the Bible, about prayer always being answered and all the possibilities of an omnipotent God being available on tap to the believer who asks in the name of Jesus (John 14:14), so often it feels as if God has just "flewed away".

We pray about something that is vital to us and urgent, and it's as if we are speaking into a huge dark void, where nobody is listening – or worse, where nobody is interested. We expect some acknowledgement, perhaps a warm feeling of assurance, but it's not there. Why? What's the point of praying if there's no response?

There could be many reasons. Maybe we're asking for the wrong thing, or at the wrong time. God's timetable is very different from ours, so it could be: "Yes, but not yet". Perhaps our prayer focus is on ourselves when at that moment others are more important, or there is some obstacle between us and God that needs to be dealt with.

Sometimes God's answer is simply "No".

We need to remember two things. First, our prayers are always answered, in the way that is best for us. Look back on your life and there will be plenty of times when God gave answers, though we didn't recognise it at the time.

Then remember that Jesus knows what it's like. On the cross he cried: "My God, my God, why have you forsaken me?" as he stared into the huge dark void (Matthew 27:46). In Gethsemane he asked God to let him off the terrible experience to come (Matthew 26:39) and got the answer "No".

Whatever our experience of prayer, let's never give up, because he hasn't flewed away, he's always there and wants to share our joys and fears through the medium he's given us – prayer.

Yes, we can!

Once upon a time we were involved with a Toy Library for children with special needs and I attended a course on "Running a Toy Library" at Warwick University. It was both useful and fun, until it came to the practical session – creating a toy from everyday materials.

Now I am quite useless at such projects and didn't know where to start, but with advice from the course leader, a washing-up liquid bottle, a dishmop and some sticky-backed plastic I became the creator of a pop-up dolly.

Never was there such a triumph, especially since a short while later I received in the post a certificate that read: "This is to certify that Mr CJM Thomas ... made one pop-up dolly, entirely unaided, during the Toy Libraries Association Course ... on Saturday 15th September 1979" and signed by the Director. The artefact is preserved at our house for anyone to see.

Being loved by God is such a joy and privilege that we want to do things for him in return, but often we get stuck on what we can do. There are terrifying lists of spiritual gifts in Paul's epistles:

prophecy, evangelism, teaching – but what if we don't think we're capable of any of those?

Many of us firmly believe we are not cut out for such great work. I know people who really feel upset they're not making a contribution to God's work in their church or outside. But let's see – we are told we all have a gift of some sort and a part to play (1 Corinthians 12), so we need to ask God to show us what and how.

Then let's consider what we do each day and think whether God is actually using us more than we realise. And occasionally let's take a risk by having a go at talking about Jesus, or volunteering to take part in a church activity, or inviting someone to Alpha. You never know what you can do unless you've tried, especially with God's help.

There was a widow who had nothing, who gave her last few coins to God (Luke 21:1,2). We may think we're no use to God, but he knows otherwise. We offer him our nothing, and he creates something – usually something wonderful. Can we do it? Yes, with God, we can!

Who are you, again?

There's a wonderful new machine at our doctors' surgery. It measures everything – height, weight, blood pressure, Body Mass Index. Every physical characteristic laid bare. Except when my wife used it something must have gone wrong. She followed the instructions and after beeps and flashing lights it produced a little printout that read: weight 0, height 0, BP 0, BMI 0 ... let's face it, according to the machine she didn't exist. Some might find that reassuring, but it's somewhat disturbing. Does she exist? Or does the machine think her details are not worth recording?

It's easy to feel invisible and useless, especially when everybody else seems to have sparkling talent and exciting lives. Like the verses from Psalm 22: "I am a worm and not a man, scorned by men and despised by the people." Psalm 22:6

But – and it's a big but – that's the psalm Jesus quoted when he was dying on the cross: "My God, why have you forsaken me?", when he was demonstrating God's amazing love by giving up his life for our sake, just because he loves us.

Jesus talked about himself as the good shepherd, who "lays down his life for the sheep" (John 10:11) and, moreover, "calls his sheep by name" (John 10:3). His love isn't a generalised liking for sheep, but a specific care for each unique individual.

I had a colleague once who didn't like ringing her own doorbell in case she opened the door to herself, but that ain't going to happen. Despite the old legends of the "Doppelgänger", each of us is unique (as witnessed by our DNA), and God knows us and cherishes you and me. He knows us as individuals and tells us: "I have summoned you by name, and you are mine ... since you are precious and honoured in my sight ... and I love you." Isaiah 43:1,4

Ignore the machine that ignores you. You're unique. You're special. You're loved and valued for who you are.

Praise Him!

A touch of the exotic

As we walked, we met a friend heading in the same direction, and as my wife and friend chatted I picked up perhaps one word in three. She spoke of her daughter, who she said was in Burma. My interest was sparked. Majestic pagodas, crumbling monuments in impenetrable jungle, overloaded boats on the Irrawaddy – Kipling's song of the Dawn Coming Up Like Thunder.

"Which part of Burma?" I asked, and she looked puzzled. "Not Burma, Bournemouth". Oh. Suddenly the day seemed duller. Nothing against Bournemouth, mind, but it just isn't Burma.

Some folk are put off by Christianity and Church because the whole thing seems exotic, out of the ordinary, unrelated to life and experience. They think they may be expected to perform outlandish rituals more suited to a Hammer horror film than the simplicities of faith. But that's a misconception.

As the Alpha course – or any ordinary Christian – can tell us, the basics of the faith centre on a personal relationship between each one of us and God, whether we know him as Father, Jesus his Son, or the Holy Spirit, built on love. Anything else is probably what we've added because we like things to be a bit exotic.

Every Church is different in the way it celebrates and worships the wonders of God. Some will have bells, candles, incense and glorious choral singing. Others will express themselves by sitting in silence for an hour or more – and infinite variety in between. That's a blessing because it means somewhere there is a church that suits our personal way of being with God. What matters is the relationship, not the way we express it.

We just need to ensure the expression doesn't become more important to us than the relationship – see Jesus' story of the Pharisee and the tax collector in Luke 18.

Our faith is expressed in every word and action of our ordinary humdrum life. And yet it's still exciting, because of the extra dimension of God's presence and the wonderful things he's given us.

Just look at a magnificent sunset – Bournemouth becomes Burma and so much more, as exotic as you like, seen through our knowledge of God.

Engage autopilot

I'm probably too frequent a visitor to the doctors' surgery, but inevitably there's somebody else I know sitting in the waiting room. Automatically I find myself saying "Hello! How are you?" and immediately think: what a daft question! There must be something wrong or they wouldn't be there. I haven't lived here long enough to have acquired the local greeting "Y'all right?" which is even less appropriate. Also, I'm at an age when I can't remember doing things I do automatically – did I lock the door? Clean my teeth? Post that birthday card? Put the cat out? No – actually, we haven't got a cat ...

So much of what we do is on autopilot, done or said without thinking and immediately forgotten. But things of importance can get missed out because they require thought or planning or action. It may be automatic to say: "I'll pray for you", but to remember to do so needs effort.

It's automatic to ask God for help, but easy to forget to thank him when he does what we ask.

Jesus spent much of his ministry either lambasting the religious authorities for their automatic response to what they saw as ignoring (their interpretation of) God's rule book, or hammering away at his disciples so the God-inspired word or action became the first thing in their minds.

In Matthew's gospel (25:31-46) Jesus talks about how we might account for our lives before God. Those of us seen to be "righteous" feed the hungry, welcome strangers, visit the sick and people in prison, not because it's in the rule book or expected of us, not because it makes us feel better, not because it looks good on our CV, but because it's an automatic reaction when we live in the love of God. His love is so powerful we can't help sharing it with everybody else.

After all, the picture of God that Jesus paints is of a father who simply can't help loving us, his children, however we behave. It's automatic with him. How dare we be any different in our interaction with our sisters and brothers? "Hello, how are you?" then becomes a real enquiry leading to real loving action.

Engage autopilot and enjoy the flight!

Is that all there is?

Working in London for so many years, I got to know several famous squares on my lunchtime walks. One day I remember a new notice at the entrance to one such, that read DIVERSIONS AHEAD. My pace quickened – what would it be? Jugglers, acrobats, fire-eaters, clowns? Maybe a tightrope walker.

But as I turned the corner there was nothing, just a small digger burying itself in a hole. And the bright face of the Chicago Pizza Pie Factory.

I felt very flat.

"Is that all there is?" sang Peggy Lee, reviewing what should have been high points in her life.

Some of us may have felt like that soon after we became Christians, especially if we'd had a dazzling experience like Paul on the road to Damascus, zapped by the living presence of Jesus, encountering for the first time the wonderful and terrifying existence of the Living God. To go to church (perhaps also for the first time) the next Sunday, singing unfamiliar songs, being subjected to a lecture from the front – wouldn't anybody say: "Is that all there is?"

It can be disappointing to recognise we shouldn't expect such a high level of excitement to be sustained, and committing ourselves to Jesus doesn't mean the world around us has changed. Indeed Jesus promised anything but an easy life full of excitement (as Lynn Anderson sang: "I never promised you a rose garden"). Work, shopping, commuting – they aren't transformed, but we are.

So what we can do, in the newly-discovered light of God's love, is to enjoy everything about our everyday experience – one aspect of what Jesus called living life to the full. Relish the ordinary, do our very best with the unpromising material of Now and Today (not the magazines!).

To quote a rather different song, by George Herbert: "Who sweeps a room as for thy laws Makes that and the action fine". Walking with Jesus can transform the everyday into the extraordinary, and give purpose to mundane repetitive tasks.

"Is that all there is?"

Maybe it is, for now, but just see what Jesus can do with it!

What, no fail certificate?

A small girl, walking with Grandma to school, discussing playing her musical instrument in an upcoming exam, asked: "If you fail the exam, do they give you a Fail Certificate? I wouldn't like that".

I should think not! Imagine a framed Fail Certificate on the wall alongside others, a permanent reminder of how unsuccessful you were, no matter how much you practised. To see it every day, to be unable to forget how far you fell short of how you ought to have been ... it would be enough to make anyone give up.

But we tend to award ourselves Fail Certificates anyway. We don't need anyone else to pronounce a verdict on our efforts. Constantly I tell myself I ought to have said this, done that, helped that friend in trouble, kept quiet instead of shouting the odds – but I didn't, and I berate myself for my failures.

And then there's all the stuff we know God wouldn't want us to do, whether we label it "sin" or just falling short of his standards. The old image of the angel at the gate of heaven with a book recording all our bad deeds reinforces our guilt about not following God closely enough. But Jesus made it abundantly clear that if we acknowledge our inadequacy and offer it sincerely to God, then God forgives us.

Now we can forgive people who do us wrong, with a bit of effort, but if we find ourselves saying: "Of course I forgive, but I can't forget" – we issue a Fail Certificate.

Then we expect God to behave like us, forgiving but keeping it on record.

Not so! In the Letter to the Hebrews (8:12) God is quoted as saying about his people: "I will forgive their wickedness, and will remember their sins no more". The slate is wiped clean, there's no endorsement on your licence, and as we say "Oops, I did it again" we should hear God's response: "You did what again?" There's no Fail Certificate to hang on the wall.

Oh dear, I just remembered that bit in the Lord's Prayer that says "Forgive us our sins, as we forgive those who sin against us". Time to shred all the Fail Certificates I've issued.

Lamentable Intelligence from the Admiralty

The sinking of HMS *Vanguard* in 1875

Chris Thomas

Just let me do this first …

A few years ago I wrote a book and actually got it published (available at a discount, signed if you insist). Inordinately proud of my achievement, I decided to present a copy to the venerable educational institution that fostered any talent I may then have had. Off we went, my wife and I, with the book, anticipating a good day out.

As we got off the bus the heavens opened – and we had quite a long walk ahead of us. We were expected, so when we arrived soaked to the skin we were welcomed by the Librarian.

Seeing our squelchy condition, she excused herself for a moment and returned bearing a huge wad of man-sized tissues. How thoughtful!

But instead of offering them to us to wipe our dripping faces, she grabbed the book and tenderly dabbed away any traces of damp. No doubt at all as to where her priorities lay. So we wandered away, satisfied that my creation was in the hands of someone who would look after it properly.

At work or in the home we start each day full of ideas on how it should go, and probably end each day wondering why it didn't. We're constantly bombarded by unexpected demands, all needing immediate attention, and unless we really know our priorities and stick firmly to them, everything becomes a mishmash of unfulfilled intentions.

The evangelist J John has said: "If we don't live by priorities, we will live by pressures". That way lies a sense of failure, confusion, depression, losing touch with God.

But if we make God and his guidance our first priority, aren't we in danger of losing touch with what we call "the real world"?

Not at all, said Jesus: "Seek first the Kingdom of God and his righteousness, and all these things will be given to you as well." Matthew 6:3

Making God our top priority means having both God's promises and a fuller, richer life here and now. Have another look at your inbox, in-tray, morning post, diary entries, to-do list, and ask yourself how to put God first.

Then he might also be satisfied his creation is in the hands of someone who will look after it properly.

I am what I eat

A local supermarket has an aisle of "Wholesome Foods". That brought me up short. Were they admitting the rest of the food was less than wholesome? It all tastes good and I know of no epidemics of food poisoning, so what can it mean?

On the shelves so labelled are mostly nuts, cereals and dried fruit, all of which are certainly healthy (unless you are allergic to nuts) and highly recommended, it appears, by dieticians and allied professionals.

The question perhaps is – should I restrict myself to Wholesome Foods in order to live a long and active life, or can I allow the occasional doughnut?

The apostle Paul's friends in the young church in Philippi were faced with a similar dilemma when they received and read a letter from him. He had much to say about living the Christian life, and towards the end added: "Finally, brothers and sisters, whatever is true, whatever is noble, whatever is right, whatever is pure, whatever is lovely, whatever is admirable — if anything is excellent or praiseworthy — think about such things." Philippians 4:8

In other words, if you want to live a full life with Jesus, think wholesome thoughts, and nothing else.

Oh dear. The problem with most of us is that controlling our thoughts seems impossible. Our thoughts express our feelings, and how often in a TV soap episode does a character say: "I can't help how I feel"?

God's standards are always beyond our reach. James wrote: "We all stumble in many ways" (James 3:2) and the only perfect person is Jesus. But as usual God meets us half way.

Through the Holy Spirit, if we really try to keep our minds off the sordid, the un-loving, the thoughts that damage us as people, God gives us a hand.

I'm told avoiding doughnuts altogether would make me lithe and slender. I know if I really try to discipline my thought life I can become closer to Jesus and a better child of God.

Wholesome brain foods, anyone?

The joke's on me

Nativity plays are one of the great joys of the Christmas season. One in particular survives in our memory, performed by children at a school for those with special needs. On to the stage erupted a small mob of shepherds, one of whom went straight to the manger and addressed the baby thus: "Nice to see you, to see you nice"! The audience were helpless with laughter, and the young shepherd was delighted they all shared his joy at meeting such an important baby.

Now, was that sacrilege, or even blasphemy? I should hope not. If the shepherd had fallen to his knees and uttered a long speech full of Thee's and Thou's he might have satisfied past generations, but he wouldn't have expressed himself naturally and with real pleasure. Nor would his hearers have been able to share the moment.

For too many ages we have suppressed the fun of the Gospel. For fear of trivialising the message we've ruled out a huge part of what it is to be human. At many points in the Bible we can share in a moment of fun, of joy, of laughter – for instance, with Abraham's wife Sarah, far too old to bear a child, who couldn't contain herself when she became pregnant. "God has brought me laughter, and everyone who hears about this will laugh with me," she said. Genesis 21:6

Jesus, the great storyteller, slipped many comic references into his parables. Just picture the man who complained about a speck in his brother's eye when he was walking around with a socking great plank in his own! Matthew 7:1-5

So it is with the Christmas story. Much of it raises a smile – scruffy shepherds receiving the full blast of an angelic choir, richly caparisoned camels bearing Wise Men picking their fastidious way through the roughest parts of Israel, wily Herod beaten at his own game ... read with laughter in mind, the story becomes even richer..

Laughter is our natural response to the unlikely, the ludicrous, the joyful.

Paul called himself "a fool for Christ" (1 Corinthians 4:10) and called us to share his foolishness. So let's thank God for his precious, healing gift of laughter and yield ourselves to it as often as we can.

Be prepared!?

It was a weekend so I was in my travelling clothes, scruffy as you like, boarding a DC-10 for the flight from one far eastern country to another.

The first surprise was that I'd been upgraded, so I sat in solitary First Class splendour for nearly three hours over featureless ocean. I disembarked, running fingers over very prickly stubble, to be met by the office driver.

As we set off, I idly asked what hotel we were heading for. "Oh no, not hotel, Mr P have party." Horrors! Sure enough, from the car I was ushered into a noisy, vigorous gathering of the finest members of the artistic establishment of this bustling capital city. And who was the guest of honour? Yes, of course, the Inspector from London. Me. Looking like a tramp.

It all happened forty years ago, but still a wave of embarrassment overwhelms me when I remember it. Of course it all went well, thanks to the tact of my good friend Mr P, but face it, I wasn't prepared, and I should have been. Such parties were our stock in trade.

Jesus made quite a thing of being prepared for his return. See the story in Matthew 25 about the ten girls waiting for the bridegroom, five of whom messed up big time because they weren't ready. In the culture of the time, they didn't just miss a very important ceremony, they were barred from a week's celebrations and all the resulting joy and excitement.

Jesus' message is: I'm coming back. I don't know when, but I can give you a hint about what it will be like. Just remember that, and be prepared!

Prepared – but how? We've got jobs to do that God has given us, relationships to cherish, everyday life to live – live to the full, promised Jesus.

Surely we're not expected to sit on the bench, ticket to heaven in hand, just waiting?

No, indeed, but it does make sense to keep the channels open, listen for God's prompting, do all we can to follow his guidance so when the time comes we can join the party and dive into the glory of God's eternity.

By the way, you're the guest of honour!

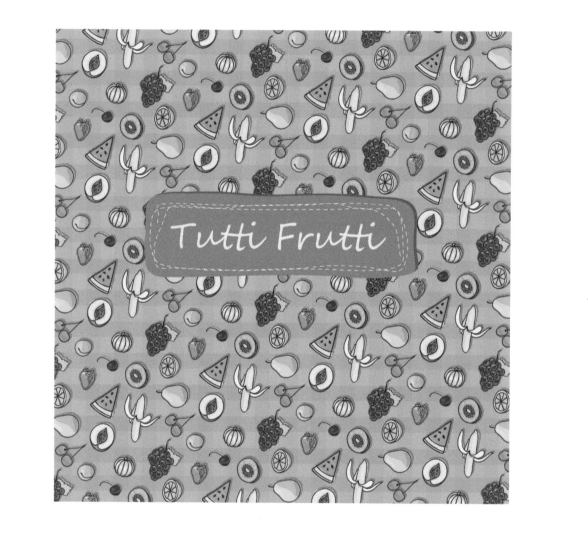

Tutti Frutti

The coffee shop where we often meet our friends was advertising a new range and using the line from Little Richard's "Tutti Frutti" that goes "Wop bop a-loo bop a-lop bom bom". Except they'd spelt it wrong. I was all for berating the management, but realised it wasn't their fault, it came from head office.

Such sloppy use of time-honoured lyrics offended me. They might have taken the trouble to get it right. Or so I thought, until I looked it up on the internet, which of course didn't exist when the song and its many cover versions were first recorded. Some start with "Hey", others end with "a-wop bamboo". The variations are many and inventive. So does it matter?

Some people coming to meet Jesus in church, home group or quietly at home worry about getting it right. My father was Chapel and my mother High Church and he found it impossible to remember when to sit, kneel or stand in a service – so he just did what seemed right at the time.

There is a story in John's gospel (chapter 4) about Jesus meeting a woman who asked whether it was right to worship God on a particular mountain or in Jerusalem. Jesus answered, in effect, that it didn't matter. What counted was that you worshipped "in spirit and in truth".

There are perhaps as many ways of worshipping or relating to God as there are Christians. Even though we may specify particular forms of words for certain Church services, what God wants is for us to be sincere and committed in working on our relationship with him.

Another story Jesus told is in Luke chapter 18:9 onwards, about a religious type who made sure he got his worship word-perfect compared with an ordinary bloke who just prayed: "God, have mercy on me, a sinner". "I tell you," said Jesus, "that this (i.e. the second) man, rather than the other, went home justified before God."

Let's not worry about getting it just right, let's put all we've got into it and really mean it.

A small exercise – stand up, take a deep breath, and belt out the lyrics to "Tutti Frutti". Now how do you feel? And did it matter how it was spelt?

Who needs a tail, anyway?

We were all attending a Christian gathering in Somerset and the speaker announced one of those unspeakably embarrassing 'getting to know you' moments. "Pretend to be your favourite animal" she said. There ensued roars, bleats, yelps, trumpeting – bedlam. I made no noise, but spread my fingers and flickered my tongue in and out, to the family's bafflement. Eventually I had to explain – of course, I was being a gecko.

Walls and ceilings throughout the world's warm countries are the little lizard's happy hunting ground, where a decent lunch consists of a few fresh mosquitoes and other creepy-crawlies, many of them noxious to you and me. The gecko is invaluable to us, and where he reigns supreme we can feel safer from disease. Yet he wears his importance lightly, has no airs and graces. He's just there, unobtrusive, mostly ignored, doing his job.

The humble gecko. We can learn from him. In any organisation, churches included, it's nice to be given a title and status and a huge temptation to make the most of them (did I tell you I'm to become 'Reader Emeritus' in the Autumn?).

Jesus, the one person in the world who deserved to be looked up to as "Wonderful, Counsellor, Mighty God" and such (Isaiah 9:6) said: "The greatest among you should be like the youngest, and the one who rules like the one who serves." Luke 22:26

That doesn't fit well into our human society. Many looked askance when a management guru wrote in the 1970s that people in senior management should regard themselves as servants of the workforce. But it's highly preferable to insisting on the rights conferred by one's status.

"God opposes the proud but gives grace to the humble." 1 Peter 5:5

Pride implies doing things my way rather than God's, and humility means putting God and other people first.

The gecko, if it loses its tail, can grow another one – so what if the tail was its pride and joy? Let's try not to rely too much on titles and trappings. Who needs a tail anyway?

By the way, you needn't always call me 'Emeritus'.

Let's fast-forward this bit

There's an anecdote I've been trying to track down about one of the very musical Strauss family. It tells how he had a great fear of the uncontrolled vigour of nature, preferring the predictable and ordered city – so much so that when he travelled from Vienna to Linz he would sit on the floor of the railway carriage with his back to the window, to avoid seeing the green landscape rushing by.

I feel something of this watching the television news. Every item carries the menace of imminent chaos. War in strange places, murder on one's doorstep, corruption in unlikely quarters, all out of my control, threatening to overwhelm all I've worked for and believe in.

Some people turn to the Church in the hope of finding stability and safety in a well-ordered world. Well, we try to organise our church lives in our human way. We sing the same songs, often repeat the same prayers, follow a calendar that tells us precisely where we are in time, all because we worship a God of order.

See in the very beginning of the Bible how he took somewhere that was "formless and empty" (Genesis 1:2) and transformed it into a paradise to be home for his friend, mankind.

God is utterly dependable. He does what he promises.

But the threat of the wildwood is still there. There is evil in the world. Peter wrote: "the Devil prowls around like a roaring lion." 1 Peter 5:6

We need to keep in touch constantly with the safe sanctuary of God, remembering Jesus said: "In this world you will have trouble. But take heart! I have overcome the world." John 16:33

And there's more – we ask to be filled with the Holy Spirit, but do we really understand what we're taking on, or what he might do with us?

"The wind blows wherever it pleases" said Jesus, talking about the Spirit (John 3:8). If you want a quiet life, don't become a Christian.

We can't fast-forward the awkward or uncontrollable bits of life, but we can hand them over to God to keep us safe and make good out of chaos. Go on, look out of the window – and see what God can do!

The green gene

There are many good things about the Muppets, despite my small son's reaction to their appearance on the TV screen: "Go 'way!" he said loudly. Brightly coloured monsters didn't appeal, nor did the battered romance between Kermit the Frog and Miss Piggy. To me however they remain full of good things.

Once many years ago, before the advent of CDs or digital streaming, I wanted the lyrics of a Muppet song and had to find the sheet music. No luck, until I rang the Jim Henson organisation direct. Bless them, they were intrigued by the idea of the song featuring in a sermon, and sent me a free copy. The song was, and is, "Bein' Green".

"It's not that easy bein' green," sang Kermit, reflectively, blending into the green background. He listed the disadvantages, but found positive things to balance them.

Maybe for some that's like becoming a Christian. We join the green club full of people like ourselves who give comfort and reassurance, and try not to think of the opportunities to be like the "flashy sparkles" we may have given up.

But we have to face the fact that we are undeniably green, and not like most of the rest of the world. For Kermit, there is no choice. He was born that way.

For us, we have to make a conscious decision, eyes wide open to the consequences, the responsibilities, the glorious privileges. We need deliberately to "take off our old self" (Colossians 3:9) and assume a new identity that involves being green, being different, perhaps renouncing fame as the world sees it but accepting there can be immense fulfilment in loving who we are and where we are, with God.

Being green can lay us open to ridicule, or to the assumption we have weird ideas that make us somehow lesser people. What we may have given up in order to become green is insignificant compared with what we will have gained. So Kermit sings: "I am green, and it'll do fine, it's beautiful, and I think it's what I want to be".

Me, too!

Follow the recipe – if it makes sense

The curate's young wife took her implied duties as a 'member of staff' very seriously, and found there just wasn't enough time to do all she thought she ought to be doing. Thus it was she turned up at the home-group looking flustered but ready to study the Word.

"So sorry I'm late," she said, "It's that fruit cake. It's taken me twice as long to bake as I expected". Under further questioning she explained "Well, the recipe said 'halve the fruit', and it's so fiddly to cut each raisin and currant in half ..."

How far do we take the principle that the Bible text is literally true and should be followed to the letter?

I'm not going to attempt to examine that huge question, but suggest we can adopt an approach that leaves room for several different ways of coming to the written word we acknowledge as God's manual for life.

First, there's the problem of translation. The scholars who produced the various versions and English translations over the past 500 years worked in widely differing cultures, and with developing understanding of the languages they worked with. It can help to have access to a variety of versions, to get a 3D picture of what the original text might have meant.

Then there's interpretation. A friend once told me he didn't give to charity because Jesus said "The poor you will always have with you" (Matthew 26:11), so we couldn't do anything about poverty. Read that verse, and it's obvious Jesus meant nothing of the sort!

To me it seems each of us needs to work towards an understanding of what the text means for us, personally. That is, what God wants to say to you and me, today.

Setting out on this journey, we need to spend time reading the Bible, discussing it with other Christians, consulting commentaries, and above all praying to God to help us understand, accept, and do what he wants. That way the recipe becomes clearer each day!

The sound of silence

The wonderful film director David Lean appeared (in archive film) on television a few weeks ago. He talked about his craft with the enthusiasm and irritation of a perfectionist, at one point saying sharply "Dialogue to me is a bore."

Horrors! What about the scriptwriters, the sound engineers, the actors laboriously learning lines? Film without dialogue is inconceivable in the 21st century, surely? Well, of course the Director's primary concern is the 'Mise-en-scène', the totality of what appears in each frame, so the story is told by what the viewer sees rather than hears. Dialogue could indeed be a distraction.

Do words get in the way when we try to communicate with God? Do we let him get a word in edgewise? Do we actually need words at all?

Me, I'm a great fan of silence. Real silence, not the times when someone plays quiet music that's supposed to help but which some people find interferes with concentration.

Jesus often deliberately sought solitude and silence at important times in his life. Preparing for his ministry he went into the desert, that vast temple of silence where all you hear is the wind – and, in his case, the tempting whisper of Satan. Throughout his ministry, and especially just before his arrest and execution, he left his disciples to be alone with God, usually (we might assume) in silence.

God has so much he wants to share with us, and we have so many competing demands on our time in this madly communicating age. Silence is precious but we've let it slip through our hands, and with it many opportunities to deepen our relationship with God.

If it were not for silence, how would Elijah have heard the 'gentle whisper' (1 Kings 19:12) that sent him on the next stage of his mission?

Maybe we need to seek out moments of silence, build them into our day, so not only may we unload all we wish for on to God, but he can have a proper chance to spell out his will for us.

There is no need to be afraid of silence. Comfort, strength, reassurance, inspiration, excitement and more can be found in the bottomless silence of the close presence of God.

What do you mean, "old"?

A friend of ours, now well into her ninth decade, was waiting for her husband in the supermarket when she heard a mother saying to a small child: "They're over there by that old lady". For a moment it didn't register. Then came the awful realisation that SHE was "that old lady".

When did that happen, when is someone suddenly been seen by the world as "old"? The problems arise from other people's assumptions about old folk, and our own expectations of our contribution to society.

To start with, we should remember no matter how wrinkly we may look on the outside, God's interested in how we are inside: "Man looks at the outward appearance, but the Lord looks at the heart." 1 Samuel 16:7

What we look like gets us pigeon-holed immediately by many people, in whose lexicon 'wrinkles' mean 'old' which means 'useless'.

God doesn't work like that. He has given each of us unique gifts, which he expects us to develop and use in his service, and age doesn't enter into the contract at any point. Indeed it can be an enhancing factor: "Grey hair is a crown of splendour." Proverbs 20:29

The elderly members of a church family should be "temperate, worthy of respect, self-controlled, and sound in faith, in love and in endurance" (Titus 2:2), a source of wisdom, continuity, calm, strength. Hardly useless!

Unfortunately we tend to expect too little of ourselves. We too assume that old equals incapable. But if we physically can't go to relieve suffering in war-torn areas of the world, we can still pray, offer hospitality, listen to those who need to talk. Because whatever the condition of body or brain might be, God's love is the same for all of us, and his promises remain valid.

"Even in your old age and grey hairs, I am he who will sustain you. I have made you and I will carry you; I will sustain you and I will rescue you." Isaiah 46:4

God grant that as I approach my eighties I shall continue to have the assurance to say "Yes, I'm old; so let's go for it!"

More tea, Vicar?

When I started work in the late 1950s my employers looked after the welfare of the hundreds of overseas students in the UK. They produced a little red booklet called "How to Live in Britain", with useful tips about the opening hours of shops, the cost of a rail ticket from Liverpool to London (£2 4s 6d or £2.22½) and so on.

Under the heading "Accepting Hospitality" in the 1962 edition appears the following injunction: "If your invitation is for, say, 4.30 pm, you should take leave of your hosts not later than 6.15 pm, unless you are pressed to stay."

Were the British ever so rigidly timetabled? I don't remember such a firmly established social structure, with Afternoon Tea at predetermined times – although my mother liked to deploy her cake stand for selected guests. Nowadays, of course, life is much less formal, and perhaps the better for it.

We are much less formal in our relationship with God, too. However much some may miss the rich wording of Holy Communion (1662), the way to meet God is undoubtedly more user-friendly for many of us in our various worship services. Nevertheless, we should try to avoid getting into a God-rut in which we expect the Creator to fit into our limited horizons, Jesus to heal just the people we like, and the Holy Spirit to come when called like a well-bred poodle. God can't be constrained by anybody's timetable but his own, which is beyond our understanding.

In particular the Holy Spirit, sent to live as God in us, is our closest friend and guide, but cannot be boxed in: "The wind blows wherever it pleases. You hear its sound, but you cannot tell where it comes from or where it is going. So it is with everyone born of the Spirit" said Jesus (John 3:8).

We need to timetable our lives, because the society we live in and our own daily routine both require structure. Hopefully, we won't try to box God in by demanding he fits into our flimsy schedule.

Oh dear, I used the word "hopefully". After 65 years or more my old English teacher's stern verdict still makes me flinch: "There is no such word!" I could just do with one of my mother's Welshcakes, but it's not yet half past four …

Taste and see

In my youth Christmas time often involved invitations to acquaintances with whom we had little contact during the rest of the year.

One such was an elderly widow whose house betrayed her Victorian tastes – today the words 'gloomy' and 'cluttered' would come to mind. We sat stiff-backed while she bustled about preparing tea and mince pies, the latter of course homemade (no handy supermarkets then).

The plate of mince pies circulated and she left the room to get the teapot. My father took a generous bite of pastry, and froze. In a stage whisper he said "It's chutney!" and we hurriedly swapped pies for chunks of Christmas cake. It must have been dark in the larder, and you couldn't but be sorry for our hostess after our departure, when she saw her hard work of baking appeared to have been rejected.

What you try for the first time may be a shock to the taste-buds but is rarely fatal. But by avoiding new tastes we risk missing something wonderful. We are creatures of habit and don't trust the unfamiliar.

Remember the old slogan advertising a brand of stout: "I've never tried it because I don't like it"? Children reject unfamiliar vegetables (or perhaps any vegetables), and need to have their palates educated. So do we, if we have studiously avoided anything to do with God because "I've never tried it ..."

The psalmist said: "Taste and see that the Lord is good" (Psalm 34:8), and the experience of so many is that to dare to taste is to experience a whole new world of joys that otherwise we'd not know existed. A rainbow explosion of richness makes life suddenly worth living in the fullest sense.

This is equally true for those of us who have been Christians for many years but are reluctant to step outside a familiar mode of worship. If we refuse to taste the new recipes, how can we know whether they will enhance our relationship with God or not? If they turn out (to our taste) to be chutney, so be it. Each of us must relate to God in our own way.

But let's have a taste – please!

A faint smile

I have mentioned before a little booklet produced by my employers in the 1960s to help overseas students settle into British society. To ensure a good beginning to relationships, it had this to say about first encounters: "When British people are introduced to each other, they give a faint smile and say 'How do you do?'".

The next paragraph starts with "The British are said to be hard to get to know". Oh, the hours I've spent practising that faint smile – and still it comes over as a manic grin. Where did we get this reputation for stiffness and formality? Surely things have changed in the past sixty years?

My theory (which you may not have sought but are going to get anyway) is that our nation has a deep-seated terror of dealing with new people, a fear of giving too much away, of getting "involved" and out of our depth, of embarrassment, of losing control. Therefore we constructed a set of greetings that kept people at arm's length until we knew they were safe to be with.

And we have a similar problem with God. We don't know how to talk to him, we desperately want to get it right but we're afraid of getting drawn in, becoming too involved, acquiring fearsome new commitments.

The problem is that establishing a relationship with God isn't just a matter of love and intimacy, it requires total commitment of all we are. "Put off your old self ... to be made new ... and put on the new self, created to be like God." Ephesians 4:22-24

We just don't like to submit, to hand over our skills and achievements and self-respect, effectively to lose control of our lives. The 1980s taught us to look after Number One, not to let anyone get the better of us – but here's our Creator and friend asking for everything we have made of ourselves. Yet the rewards for giving ourselves away are so astounding it's not worth thinking twice about it.

There's eternal life, for a start. Not an endless life of drudgery but a full and rich experience infused with the relationship between each one of us and God.

No faint smiles for me, mate – I'm for grabbing at it with both hands, yes please!

Reciprocal communication strategy

"Beg parding, Mrs Harding, is my kitting in your garding?" Do you recognise that? I'm told it's a nursery rhyme, but for the life of me I can't remember ever having heard it used to soothe or stimulate denizens of the nursery – and yet it's stuck fast in my memory. But what does it mean? And why was it (presumably) popular enough to be handed down the generations?

I suspect children enjoy it because it's like a secret language, understandable only to a small circle, showing that if you know it you're part of a special group and probably superior to non-members.

Every trade, profession and secret society has its jargon. When I was an air cadet it was back-slang, and I was known as "Ornhay Imeray" because of the horn-rimmed spectacles I wore.

Church members aren't exempt from the urge to be thought different from the mob. We may not use words like hermeneutics or eschatology in everyday parlance, but what about grace, repentance, sin, saviour? I dare you to define them so they're easily understood by the person next to you in the checkout queue!

Jesus didn't wrap up the mysteries of the faith in impenetrable language. He emphasised the simplicity of his message and the need to respond with equal simplicity.

"Let the little children come to me ... I tell you the truth, anyone who will not receive the Kingdom of God like a little child will never enter it." Mark 10:14,15

Rather than creating a special language to demonstrate how different we believers are from the common people, we need to be open and clear about what the Christian life means to us personally so others can understand it in the simplest terms. Of course there are mysteries we can't understand at first, but the best way to get closer to their meaning is to get closer to the living Jesus. Knowing him is all we need, and living with him means we're special anyway and don't need jargon to prove it.

Incidentally the kitting was in Mrs H's garding, and chewing on a mutting bone, so that's all right, then.

Slip into something comfortable

Order one thing online and you set in train a rush of adverts offering more of the same. One caught my attention. It offered "effortless summer wear". I think I approve of that. The last thing one wants is clothing that requires focussed concentration.

The height of effortlessness appears in the Aardman cartoon "The Wrong Trousers". Wallace makes use of a sophisticated machine to get himself fully trousered without lifting a finger. In theory that should mean he has so much more time and energy to spare for the business of living.

In practice, however, there's not much in life that is entirely effortless.

We have the promise of eternal life, freedom from the captivity of sin, deep joy, and so much more that is impossible to take in – without any effort on our part. All we have to do is say "yes" to Jesus. It can be a huge comfort, as the American spiritual has it: "All my trials, Lord, soon be over". With the minimal effort of acknowledging our sinfulness, asking for forgiveness and handing ourselves over to God, everything falls into place, and we can relax in God's care.

Some people reckon that's the attraction of faith – shoving all responsibility on to God and blaming him if things don't work out. "The opium of the people" was Karl Marx's summary description. But it's not as easy as that.

First, God's promise requires our signature on the contract, showing we agree to play our part as what Paul calls: "God's fellow-workers." (1 Corinthians 3:9). In accepting God's love and grace we accept our responsibility to work with him towards the ideal world that forms part of the Kingdom of God.

Moreover, when we experience God's goodness surely we can't help doing good for the benefit of others? The prophet Jeremiah wrote God's "word is in my heart like a fire ... I am weary of holding it in" (Jeremiah 20:9). So relaxation may not be on the agenda after all.

Mind you, the thought of unloading all my sins and troubles ("O rest in the Lord" – Psalm 37:7) is very attractive. I think I'll just sit down for a minute – to acquire a bit more time and energy to spend in God's service, of course ...

There's a moose loose aboot the hoose

It was the holiday of a lifetime, a fly-drive around New England in the Fall. Stopping by the gleaming white church in a picture-postcard village, we got talking to a man who was collecting acorns to feed the chipmunks (or so he said). He told us about his son's recent marriage, and how the couple had gone to Canada on honeymoon, because the bride had always wanted to see a moose. They combed the countryside for miles in every direction, but came away disappointed. Not a single moose to be seen. Tired, they drew up outside the marital home and – you guessed it – there was a moose in their back yard, grinning a welcome (in so far as a moose can grin).

How far would you go to see a moose? Or to gratify your dearest wish?

Serious bird watchers will travel halfway round the globe to see a rare species, whether to gaze in wonder at God's creation or to tick it off their list. They'll be working from a detailed description (such as "Large brown animal with antlers and a lugubrious expression"). They'll know precisely where to look and seeking becomes their passion.

How hard do we look for Jesus? It used to be fashionable to say everybody had a "God-shaped hole" that yearned to be filled – but the new atheism doesn't allow for such fancies.

We need to be aware of how important it is to meet and follow Jesus, how to recognise his presence, and where he is to be found.

Do we start in church?

Perhaps, but don't rule anywhere out.

Do we expect a bearded, tanned figure in a white cloak?

Let's not be so restrictive.

What priority should we give the search?

"Seek first His kingdom and His righteousness" (Matthew 6:33), and all else that we wish for will follow.

Look for the moose in the back yard. It's so simple and so rewarding.

Good heavens!

Small children often produce the most illuminating thoughts about our world. One such, talking about heaven and remembering an old-fashioned Sunday School chorus, said firmly: "If all they do is sing 'Joy, Joy, Joy!' all the time, I don't want to go there".

I have some sympathy with that viewpoint. Another opinion from an older person was she didn't fancy heaven if it meant having to get on with all the people she'd disliked on earth.

Whatever your view, the practical realisation of what we expect from heaven raises some difficulties. If we're committed to the Christian faith, we look forward to the fulfilment of God's promises in a new life with him after our earthly death, in a place called heaven but what's it going to be like?

The book of Revelation has some wonderful passages about the glories to be found there, but the rich language can be confusing and we may end up none the wiser.

Let's face it – we can't know in detail what it will be like. It will surpass our imagining, nothing that worries us here will have any significance, all that troubles us now (pain, suffering, loss, sin – make your own list) will disappear and we shall be forever in the presence of God (Revelation 21:3,4).

To me, the best modern statement of what we can expect is summed up in this little poem by the late Evangeline Paterson:

> and that will be heaven
> and that will be heaven
> at last the first unclouded
> seeing
>   to stand like the sunflower
> turned full face to the sun drenched
> with light in the still centre
> held while the circling planets
> hum with an utter joy
>   seeing and knowing
> at last in every particle
> seen and known and not turning
> away
>   never turning away
> again

Maybe we'll actually want to sing "Joy! Joy! Joy!" after all?

Green fingers

The rose bed made a brave display, a barrage of floribundas that loved the Kentish clay in our old garden. Of course there was feeding and pruning and dead-heading, but the effort was worthwhile. Weeding, too.

But I was brought up short one day when a delicate feathery growth of leaves appeared to be better than weed-quality, so I left it. It grew, feminine among the butch rose bushes, a lovely contrast, an ornate addition to the display. Eventually it was clear that its time was up, so I tugged at the stem and out it came.

It was a carrot. Just one carrot, but for a while it had made our garden lovelier than expected. Growing in the wrong place, but who cared, if it was beautiful?

I had no part in its impact – it grew all by itself, knowing just what it could do and doing it to the best of its ability.

I realise I'm in danger of attributing human thoughts to a vegetable, but it struck me my carrot's life reflected that of so many of us – we may end up in the wrong place, have no obvious role in society, but that shouldn't stop us being who we are, doing what we're designed to do, in our small way making life beautiful.

The Bible is full of gifted characters, such as Bezalel the goldsmith (Exodus 31) who used his gift at God's command in building the Tabernacle to God's glory. But also Martha of Bethany, whose very ordinary gifts of running a household still made her indispensable to Jesus for those moments of relaxation during his high-pressure ministry (Luke 10:38 and following).

Bezalel wrought beauty with his hands. Martha made way for beauty by being herself and making that self open to what God required.

For all the obviously talented roses among us there are many more carrots, but never think we carrots have no value. All God asks of us is that we give ourselves to him and go on being the ordinary, complicated, beautiful people whom he made in his own image.

By the way, the carrot is a versatile vegetable – it'll go with anything. Are you ready for the adventure of being a carrot for God?

Know thyself

Recently I came across an old newspaper cutting that read: "President Amin of Uganda has asked his intelligence service to investigate him so that he can be informed of any weaknesses".

For once the long-gone tyrant (whose thugs beat up a colleague of mine) was talking sense.

How well do I know myself? What are my weaknesses? I have no doubt plenty of people would reel off a string of unsatisfactory characteristics if asked ...

We go through life blissfully unaware of the impression we're making on others, though a few moments quiet self-analysis might make all the difference in our relationships and consequently make life easier for us and for those we know and love.

In particular there's our relationship with God. We're supposed to be offering ourselves entirely to him as loving and dutiful children, but what are we actually offering? Is the package we construct fully comprehensive, or are there things we know need attention but we'd rather keep tucked out of the way because they are too difficult or indeed too enjoyable to do something about? We may not know ourselves, but instinctively we know how to bamboozle our conscience into believing a particular unacceptable activity is all right really because ...

It takes courage and a high degree of self-awareness to offer God our true unadorned selves, but that's what he wants from us, so he can take the real Me and infuse all our gifts and all our weaknesses with the power, authority and sheer overwhelming love of the Holy Spirit, for the benefit of those around us and, as it happens, of ourselves.

"Search me, O God, and know my heart!" sang the psalmist, "Try me and know my thoughts!" Psalm 139:23

I dread to think what might have happened to any of Amin's intelligence officers if they had discovered a weakness and dared tell him about it. God, on the other hand, has a habit of asking us to be totally frank with him and then turning weakness into opportunity.

Now that's what I call a constructive relationship.

A bridge too far

I have a press cutting about the return to Paris of a distinguished writer in his 70s, which says he: "returned to his old stomping grounds ... with an enchanting 29-year-old Japanese bridge."

Now I've seen many pretty, even perhaps enchanting bridges, but have never thought of them as being cuddly, or susceptible to the attractions of a "sugar Daddy".

Maybe what he showed off proudly was a bride rather than a bridge? Yet there are surely people to whom a bridge is a thing of extraordinary beauty and worthy of tender loving care. The Iron Bridge in Shropshire could be an example. Bridge devotees will go out of their way to visit an exceptional design, pay huge sums for a rare picture of the bridge under construction, sacrifice time and emotion and resources to making bridges the centre of their lives.

It had never occurred to me that a bridge could come between me and God, but certainly dedication of one's life to anything carries the risk of making it the most important part of life.

In the commandment to refrain from worshipping idols (Exodus 20:4) we are told not to put money, sex, power, self-interest and similar great concepts ahead of God in our affections, but not many of us are in a position to wield power or worship money.

The evil one (as Jesus called the force that tries to separate us from God – Matthew 6:13) is much more subtle. Do we like to keep the house spick-and-span before anything else? How about collecting fine china? Clay pigeon shooting? Nothing wrong with these things in themselves, but beware when they take over and get in the way of our relationship with God. Of course, we can go further. It's not just the old adage "Whatever you're doing, stop it". A bridge is intended as a means of joining one place to another, overriding what might be impossible obstacles. When we look hard into ourselves and identify what we "worship" we can ask God to take it from us and return it as something new and powerful, a worthy tool in building the Kingdom. He can do what we can't.

There's never a bridge so far he can't use it if we but let him.

Whistle while you work

It's 1980 and President Machel of Mozambique is addressing his people about the economy. The press later reports: "The President spoke for four and a half hours in intermittent rain to a crowd of 50,000 ... He interrupted his speech to sing, whistle, tell jokes, and compliment ministers on their clothes, but the speech itself was serious and ... of direct concern to his audience." Well, you need some light relief if you're standing in Independence Square for the length of two feature films! And the President clearly knew two things: the tolerance level of his audience, and how to express his unique personality to best effect.

When we are trying to explain the huge importance of knowing Jesus Christ and committing ourselves to him, it's tempting to think all we have to do is present the message just as we were told and the words themselves will do their work.

To some extent that's true, because if we've prayed about it and given the Holy Spirit free rein, he will certainly get going. But we need to do our share. Our listeners should be able to recognise the real 'me' in what we say, not just the Gospel recited parrot-fashion. If that involves singing, whistling and telling jokes, that's OK – provided that's who we are. We don't need to put on an act when we talk about our experience of our faith.

But we also should consider the situation of those to whom we're talking. It's worth reminding ourselves of the way Jesus related to people. At times he was tough and uncompromising (John 4), at others gentle and compassionate (Mark 5:35 on), recognising how much his audience could cope with at that point in their lives.

An exam question for you – before Alpha Course was invented there was a video series in the first of which the amateur evangelist was visited by a plumber. With the tradesman safely corralled in the loft, our hero popped his head up through the trapdoor and said "Have you been washed in the Blood of the Lamb?" Questions – (a) What did the plumber say? (b) Was this the right time and place? (c) What would you have said or done that was different? (d) What would Jesus do? (On no account write on both sides of the paper at once.)

What's in a name?

It's 1972 and I'm embarking on the last leg of a wearisome journey to Kathmandu. As we take off from Delhi, there comes the cabin crew's usual announcement: "Welcome aboard Royal Nepal Airlines Boeing 727 Yeti".

Yeti? The 727 may have a more portly profile than its fellow svelte airliners, but why give it the name of a reportedly hairy monster that leaves footprints all over the Himalayas? There is so much more in Nepal that is beautiful and graceful and impressive. Such a name seems aggressively inappropriate.

Names matter. Think of a name and you conjure up a complete person, outward appearance, character and personality. That's perhaps why names matter so much in the Old Testament. And in the New Testament Jesus can change Simon's name to Peter because he'd become a different person (Matthew 16:18).

To know and use a name is part of the essence of a relationship. Jesus says the good shepherd: "calls his own sheep by name" (John 10:3), just as the prophet Isaiah quotes God as saying "Fear not ... I have called you by name, you are mine." Isaiah 43:1

Even the Ten Commandments refer to a name: "You shall not misuse the name of the Lord your God." Exodus 20:7

I don't think I have ever heard a sermon about that Commandment, possibly because knowing a name has less or different significance nowadays. But how much does it matter? Socially, it still does. To make fun of a name or use it in an unpleasant context means you're denigrating the person named, saying they are worthless, belittling them.

The name of God is used in the 21st century as a casual swearword. Someone drops something and immediately says "God!", not in prayer but as a mild curse. Postings on social media are littered with "OMG!". For people who don't know God personally, it's unimportant, but for those who do, maybe we should pay more attention to the third Commandment and rescue the Name of our God from jokes and abuse and being dragged in the mud, paying him the respect he is due.

"Yeti" was a beautiful machine with the wrong name. Should we put up with our God being labelled "The Abominable No-Man"?

Can I get an upgrade?

Giving blood is always a tense experience and awaiting your turn at the hospital can take a long time. Our local service uses a machine that gives you a ticket showing your position in the queue. Number 45? Only 20 or so people ahead of me, so maybe an hour to wait.

But there is something printed on the ticket that undermines it all. It reads "Some tickets may be called before others".

Eh? If numbers are being called at random, what's the point of the ticket? I suppose there may be emergency patients who need to jump the queue, but it adds an unwelcome note of uncertainty, which some find irritating, others disturbing. Some indeed feel Something Must Be Done.

So it was with the mother of Jesus' disciples James and John, who went to Jesus to ask if her boys might have privileged places in the Kingdom of Heaven (Matthew 20:20 onwards). Jesus tried to explain she'd got it all wrong: "Whoever wants to become great among you must be your servant".

Another time he realised his friends had been arguing about who was the greatest – to which he again said: "If anyone wants to be first, he must be the very last." Mark 9:33 onwards.

So what's the point of throwing yourself wholeheartedly into following Jesus? Why try to be the best worshipper if your efforts go unrecognised? Time and time again Jesus makes the same point: conventional human expectations of a reward for good behaviour and hard work don't apply in God's new world.

He told a story (Matthew 20:1-16) about a boss who hired workers for periods from a full day to one hour, but paid each of them the same amount regardless of the time spent on the job.

So it's not a matter of trying to be Holier Than Thou or praying twice as hard. We are all equal in God's sight and all he wants is our acknowledgement of failure, our commitment and our love, so we can all share in the unimaginable blessings he promises.

Similarly, it's not up to us to decide which of our churchgoing friends is "a better Christian". Some numbers may be called before others, and it's his call, not ours.

Happy Dog – an update

One of the earliest in this series of little items for the Church website was about Happy Dog, the name we'd given to a particularly cheerful dog whose walk took him past our house each morning. He was a lovely illustration of the joy we can find in life if we just let God be in charge and allow ourselves to appreciate what God has done, is doing and will do with and for us.

Happy Dog came past again today, some ten dog-years older than when I first wrote about him. He may be broader in the beam, possibly a little slower, but he's still insatiably curious, delighting in smells old and new, supremely happy in the safety of being with his master and in the excitement of fresh possibilities.

Too often we can feel weighed down with the sheer unrelenting busyness of life. The same old routines, the same people saying the same daft things, the weariness of striving for a goal that seems as far away as ever. The eruption of joy when we first met Jesus has faded to a glowing ember.

Jesus himself must have felt much the same, what with outright opposition from the religious authorities and the persistent dozy ignorance of the man (and occasionally woman) in the street. But he had an answer, which we might call perseverance. The writer to the Hebrews puts it thus: "Let us run with perseverance the race marked out for us." Hebrews 12:1-8

That doesn't mean "snap out of it", which we usually can't do on our own, but taking time to pray, read the Bible, talk to friends who know us well – oh, and pray again – thereby tapping into the boundless resources and power of the Holy Spirit living in us. If we but put in a little effort the Spirit can work miracles great and small. If we haven't got the strength even to do that, we may need to let others carry us under the Spirit's guidance. It's worth it. Paul wrote: "suffering produces perseverance, perseverance, character; and character, hope." Romans 5:4

Hope brings out the joy in the Happy Dog that we all aspire to be.

I've said it before, and I'll say it again: Woof!

Image credits

Lightning Source UK Ltd.
Milton Keynes UK
UKHW021216240821
389338UK00004B/85